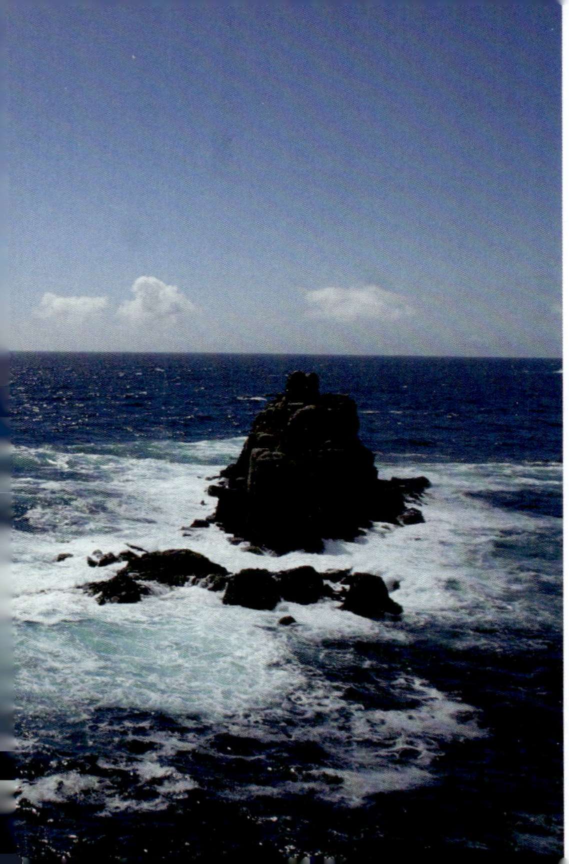

FISH RECIPES

A harvest from home waters

Dorrigo

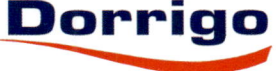

Index

Baked Brill 39
Baked Mussels 14
Brixham Fish Soup 10
Buttered Crab 38
Buttered Lobster 24
Conger Eel in Cider 7
Crab Soup 47
Crab Tart 42
Creamed Prawns 27
Cream of Scallop Soup 40
Dorset Scalloped Crab 16
Fillets of Sole in Cream Sauce 21
Fish Pasties 6
Hake with Onions 18
Lyme Bay Fish Pie 29
Mackerel in Gooseberry Sauce 5
Mackerel in Mustard Sauce 31
Monkfish Casserole 45
Newlyn Haddock 46
Oyster Stew Soup 23
Pilchard Hot Pot 37
Pilchard Leek Pie 11
Poached John Dory 22
Poached Turbot Steaks 3
Red Mullet Parcels 15
Roast Sea Bass 32
Sennen Cove Conger Eel 43
Shellfish Soup 30
Shrimp & Anchovy Sauce 34
Skate with Black Butter 8
Sole & Shrimp Pudding 35
Somerset Casserole 13
Star Gazey Pie 19
Stuffed Gurnard 26

Cover front: Port Isaac, Cover back: Lobster Pots
Title page: Land's End

Printed & published by Dorrigo, Manchester, England © Copyright
All rights reserved. No part of this publication may be reproduced, stored in a retrieval system or transmitted, in any form or by means, electronic, mechanical, photocopying or otherwise. Recipes J Salmon Ltd

Poached Turbot Steaks

The creamy white flesh of the turbot is deliciously flavoured and is considered to be the finest of the flat fish.

4 turbot steaks (approx. 6 oz each)	6 pickled walnuts
2 oz sliced onions	Small bunch watercress, finely chopped
1 oz butter	Salt and pepper
1 oz flour	4 pickled walnuts to garnish

Put the fish steaks into a pan with the onions with enough water to cover. Bring to the boil and poach gently for about 15 minutes. Remove the turbot to a serving dish and keep warm. Strain the liquid. Melt the butter in a pan, stir in the flour and gradually stir in $1/2$ pint of the fish liquid. Mash the 6 walnuts and add to the sauce with the chopped watercress and season well. Bring to the boil, stirring continually and simmer for a few minutes to thicken. Spoon the sauce over the turbot steaks and garnish with halved pickled walnuts. Serve with crusty bread and butter. Can similarly be served cold. Serves 4.

Mackerel with Gooseberry Sauce

The combination of mackerel either fried, grilled or roasted with gooseberry sauce is very ancient, said to have been brought to England about the time of the Norman conquest.

4 mackerel   **2 oz butter**
Salt and pepper   **Gooseberry sauce**
SAUCE
½ lb gooseberries   **1 oz butter**
2 oz caster sugar   **Pinch of nutmeg**

Set oven to 350°F or Mark 4. Gut and clean the fish and place in a buttered ovenproof dish. Season with salt and pepper and dot with butter. Cover with buttered foil and bake for 20 to 30 minutes. Remove from the oven, split the fish and remove the backbones and keep hot on a serving dish. SAUCE. Top, tail and wash the gooseberries, put into a pan with just enough water to cover, bring to the boil and simmer until soft. Sieve the gooseberries or blend in a liquidiser, return the purée to the pan, stir in the sugar, butter and nutmeg, reheat and beat until smooth. Serve the fish with the hot sauce and with small new potatoes. Serves 4.

Torquay

Fish Pasties

Simple puff pastry envelopes filled with parsleyed cod.

1 lb puff pastry
FILLING

½ lb cod fillet	**Juice of ½ lemon**
1 oz butter	**1 tablespoon chopped fresh parsley**
Salt and pepper	**1 egg, beaten**

Sprigs of parsley to garnish

Set oven to 450°F or Mark 8. Grease a baking sheet. Roll out the pastry thinly on a floured surface and cut into 4 rectangles. Place on the baking sheet and keep cool while making the filling. Skin the fish and cut into small pieces. Melt the butter in a pan, add the fish, season with salt and pepper, stir in the lemon juice and chopped parsley and cook, covered, for 5 minutes, shaking the pan frequently. Remove from the heat, add half of the beaten egg and mix well. Divide the mixture on to one half of each pastry rectangle, damp the edges, fold over and seal well. Brush with the remaining egg. Bake for about 10 minutes until golden brown. Serve hot or cold, garnished with parsley. Serves 4.

Conger Eel in Cider

The conger eel is a large fish with a fearsome reputation. The flesh is white and firm and full flavoured.

3 lb conger eel fillet
½ lb onions, chopped
2 oz butter
2 oz flour
2 pints cider
Salt and pepper

Set oven to 350°F or Mark 4. Skin and bone the eel, cut into thick steaks and wash and dry thoroughly. Fry the onions in the butter in a casserole dish until golden then add the eel steaks and brown lightly. Stir in the flour and continue cooking until the flour is browned. Gradually stir in the cider and season with salt and pepper. Cover with a lid or foil and cook in the oven for 1 hour. Serve the fish in its cooking liquid, thickening with a little more flour if necessary. Serves 6.

Skate with Black Butter

The kite-shaped skate wing has flesh which comes off the bone in creamy shreds. Because of the weight of bone allow about 1/2 lb of wing for each person.

2 lb skate wings, skinned   1 oz capers, chopped
1 pint fish stock   Juice of 1/2 lemon
BLACK BUTTER
4 oz salted butter   2 tablespoons white or red wine vinegar
1 tablespoon finely chopped fresh parsley

If necessary, cut the wing(s) into equal portions. Heat the stock in a deep frying pan and poach the fish for 15 to 20 minutes. Drain the fish, arrange on a dish, sprinkle with the chopped capers and lemon juice and keep warm. To make the black butter, melt the butter in a saucepan and cook until it foams and goes nut brown. Stir in the vinegar and parsley, bring to the boil and continue boiling to reduce somewhat then pour over the fish. Serve with boiled potatoes. Serves 4.

St Michael's Mount, Cornwall

Brixham Fish Soup

This fish soup or stew which it almost resembles, can be made using any mixture of white fish according to the season and the catch. There are many variations.

2 lb mixed white fish fillets (monk fish, gurnard, cod, plaice, etc)

2 tablespoons olive oil	**1½ pints fish stock**
2 onions, sliced	**½ pint dry white wine**
2 cloves garlic, crushed	**2 bay leaves**
2 medium leeks, sliced	**Salt and pepper**
2 medium carrots, sliced thinly	**4 tablespoons, double cream**
1 large can chopped tomatoes	**1 tablespoon chopped parsley**

Heat the oil in a large saucepan, add the onions and fry until softened. Add the garlic, leeks and carrots and cook for 2 to 3 minutes. Add the tomatoes, stock, wine and bay leaves. Season and simmer for 15 minutes. Prepare the fish by cutting into bite-size pieces. Add the firm fish first (for example monk fish) and cook for 3 minutes, then add the more delicate fish (for example plaice) and cook for a further 2 or 3 minutes. Do not overcook the fish. Pour the soup into a warmed tureen, stir in the cream and sprinkle with parsley. Serves 6 to 8.

Pilchard and Leek Pie

A small, round oily fish, the pilchard is, in fact, a mature sardine. Large sardines can be used instead. Most pilchards are caught around Devon and Cornwall.

4 - 8 pilchards (or large sardines) **Salt and pepper**
8 oz shortcrust pastry **5 fl oz single cream**
4 large leeks **Beaten egg to glaze**

Set oven to 325° F or Mark 3. Roll out the pastry on a floured surface and line the bottom and sides of a pie dish, reserving sufficient for the lid. Wash the leeks and cut into 2 inch lengths. Drop into boiling water for 2 minutes to blanch, then drain well. Clean the fish and arrange the leeks and the fish in the pie dish. Season well. Damp the pastry edges and cover with a pastry lid. Glaze with beaten egg. Bake for about 50 minutes until golden brown. When cooked, carefully prise off the lid, drain off the cooking liquid and replace with the cream which should be pre-heated, but not boiled. Replace the lid and serve. Serves 4.

Somerset Casserole

A substantial lunch or supper dish of cod or haddock flavoured with cider.

2 lb cod or haddock fillet	½ pint cider
2½ oz butter	Butter for dotting
Salt and pepper	1 lb creamed mashed potatoes
4 oz mushrooms, sliced	Grated cheese for sprinkling
4 oz tomatoes, skinned and sliced	Tomato slices and parsley sprigs to garnish

SAUCE

1½ oz butter   1½ oz flour   Fish liquid

Set oven to 375° F or Mark 5. Butter an ovenproof casserole dish. Cut the fish into small cubes and arrange in the dish. Season. Add the mushrooms and tomatoes, pour over the cider and dot with butter. Cover and bake for 25 minutes. Carefully strain off the liquid. To make the sauce, melt the butter in a pan, stir in the flour and gradually stir in the fish liquid. Bring to the boil and cook for a few minutes, stirring, to thicken. Increase oven to 450°F or Mark 8. Pour the sauce over the fish in the dish. Arrange a border of mashed potato, sprinkle the fish with grated cheese and garnish with tomato slices. Return to the oven, uncovered, for the cheese to bubble and to brown. Serve garnished with parsley. Serves 4 to 6.

Baked Mussels

Although abundant and inexpensive, mussels are one of the most underrated of shell fish. Their flesh is sweet and tender.

3 lb mussels, from a reliable source, thoroughly scrubbed with 'beards' removed
3 oz butter   1 medium onion, diced $1/2$ pint dry white wine   1 bay leaf
3 sprigs thyme $1^{1}/_{2}$ lb peeled potatoes, parboiled and cut into thickish slices
Salt and freshly ground black pepper   2 cloves garlic, peeled and crushed
2 oz fresh white breadcrumbs   2 oz Cheddar cheese, finely grated

Set oven to 375° F or Mark 5. Melt 1 oz of the butter in a large pan and cook the onion until it is soft. Add the wine, bay leaf and thyme and bring to the boil. Add the mussels and cook for 5 to 10 minutes until the shells open; any which do not open *must not* be used. Remove the mussels from the liquid with a draining spoon and take them out of their shells. Butter a large ovenproof dish and place a layer of potatoes in the bottom. Season with salt and pepper, dot with garlic and add a layer of mussels. Continue with layering, ending with potatoes on top. Strain the mussel liquid over the dish and top with the breadcrumbs and cheese mixed together. Dot with the remaining butter and bake for 20 minutes until bubbling hot and crisp on top. Serve immediately with a fresh green salad. Serves 4 to 6.

Red Mullet Parcels

*All the unique and delicate flavour of this rose-coloured fish
is retained within the foil wrapping.*

**4 red mullet (8 – 10 oz each)   1 tablespoon chopped fresh parsley
Salt and pepper   2 – 3 oz button mushrooms, sliced
1 onion, finely chopped   1 tablespoon lemon juice
Lemon slices and parsley sprigs to garnish**

Set oven to 350°F or Mark 4. Clean, de-scale, wash and dry the fish well. Sprinkle the insides with salt and pepper. Mix together the chopped onion and parsley and stuff each fish. Prepare 4 squares of kitchen foil and butter well. Lay a fish on each square, place a line of mushroom slices along the side and fold up the parcel, twisting and sealing the ends. Put in a baking tin and cook in the oven for 15 to 20 minutes. Loosen the parcels carefully and transfer each fish to a hot plate, leaving all the juices in the tin. Stir in the lemon juice and then pour the liquor over the fish. Serve garnished with lemon slices and parsley sprigs. Serves 4.

Dorset Scalloped Crab

This attractive starter is served in scrubbed scallop shells.

2 medium size boiled crabs
2 – 3 anchovy fillets, chopped
2 ½ tablespoons white wine vinegar
2 oz butter
4 oz fresh white breadcrumbs
Salt and Cayenne pepper
6 scallop shells
Parsley sprigs to garnish

Set oven to 350° F or Mark 4. Remove all the crab meat from the shells and claws, mix with the chopped anchovies and put into a saucepan with the vinegar, butter and 3 oz of the breadcrumbs. Season with salt and Cayenne pepper. Heat through gently for a few minutes, stirring occasionally and then divide the mixture equally between the scallop shells. Sprinkle with the remaining breadcrumbs and brown in the oven for about 10 minutes. Serve with thin slices of buttered brown bread. Serves 6.

Hake with Onions

The flaky, white flesh of hake is very tender and has a fine flavour.
Hake is a member of the cod family.

4 hake steaks (6 – 8oz each)
½ lb sliced onions   **1 bay leaf**
2 oz butter   **Salt and pepper**
Juice of ½ lemon   **5 fl oz fish stock**

Set oven to 350º F or Mark 4. Fry the onions in half the butter until light brown and then transfer to an ovenproof dish with the lemon juice and bay leaf. Place the fish steaks on top of the onions, season with salt and pepper and dot the steaks with the remaining butter. Pour in half the stock, cover with foil and bake for 15 minutes. Remove the foil and continue baking for 5 minutes more. Transfer the fish to a serving dish and keep warm. Pour the rest of the stock into the dish and boil hard to reduce to a thick sauce. Strain around the fish and serve with new potatoes and a green vegetable. Serves 4.

Star Gazey Pie

This pie epitomises the renowned Cornish pilchard fishing industry and is particularly linked with Mousehole. The name derives from the way the fish heads overlap the sides of dish and point heavenwards.

6 pilchards (or 8 large sardines)	**1 small onion, finely chopped**
8 oz shortcrust pastry	**1 egg, beaten**
6 oz brown breadcrumbs	**3 hardboiled eggs, chopped**
1 teaspoon ground cloves	**4 teaspoons single cream**
1 teaspoon allspice	**4 tablespoons chopped parsley**
Freshly ground black pepper	**Beaten egg for glazing**

Set oven to 425º F or Mark 7. Gut, clean and bone the fish, cut off the tail fins but leave on the heads. Wash the fish, pat dry, then open out. Make the stuffing with breadcrumbs, cloves, spice and pepper, mixed with the chopped onions and bound together with beaten egg. Fill the opened fish with stuffing, close up, reshape and leave in a cool place. Grease a 9 to 10 inch flat pie-dish or pie-plate. Spread any remaining stuffing over the dish and arrange the stuffed fish like the spokes of a wheel with heads on the rim and tails in the centre. Cover with chopped hard boiled egg, cream, parsley and pepper; finish covering with the rest of the pastry and pinch the two layers firmly together between the heads but roll back the pastry round the heads to reveal their eyes gazing starwards. Brush with beaten egg. Bake for 15 minutes, reduce to 350ºF or Mark 4 and continue for a further 20 minutes until the pie is golden brown. Serves 6.

Nineteen

Fillets of Sole with Cream Sauce

Next to turbot, the Dover sole is considered to have the finest flavour of any flat fish but Torbay soles and Lemon soles are equally suitable for this rich but simple dish.

4 fillets of sole (4 – 6 oz each), skin on
Salt and pepper   Juice of ½ lemon   Chopped fresh parsley to garnish
SAUCE
2 oz butter   2 oz finely chopped onion
1½ oz flour   ½ pint fish stock   5 fl oz single cream

Set oven to 350º F or Mark 4. Well butter an ovenproof dish. Wipe the fish fillets and cut each lengthways into two strips. Tie each strip loosely into a knot and place in the dish. Season with salt and pepper and sprinkle with lemon juice. Cover with buttered greaseproof paper and bake for 10 to 15 minutes. To make the sauce, melt the butter in a pan, cook the onion gently, add the flour and gradually stir in the stock. Bring to the boil and simmer for 10 minutes. Just before serving, stir in the cream and reheat well through but do not allow to boil. To serve, carefully lift the fish fillets on to a warmed serving dish, pour over the sauce and garnish with chopped parsley. Serves 4.

Kynance Cove

Poached John Dory

This ugly fish with an enormous head has firm, white flesh with a delicate flavour. Unfortunately it can be expensive as only about one third of the fish weight can be eaten. This is a simple, cold dish for summer days.

1½ lb fillet John Dory, skin on
White wine   Lemon juice   Olive oil   Salt and white pepper

Wash and dry the fish and put into a suitable pan or flameproof dish. Cover with equal parts of white wine and water, bring to the boil and simmer very gently until tender. Leave the fish to cool in the liquid then transfer to a serving dish, cover and put into the refrigerator until required. Before serving, season with salt and pepper and serve with a green salad and a dressing made from 2 parts lemon juice and 1 part olive oil. Serves 4.

Oyster Stew Soup

The Helford River is renowned for its Native oysters and the West Country has a tradition of combining cream with fish dishes. This rich meal of a soup brings both together.

- **1¼ lb fresh or tinned oysters**
- **1 oz butter**
- **8 oz finely chopped onions**
- **5 fl oz white wine**
- **1 pint double cream**
- **2 egg yolks**
- **Salt and white pepper**
- **Cayenne pepper for sprinkling**

Roughly chop the oysters and reserve the liquid. Melt the butter in a pan and cook the onions, covered, until golden. Add the wine and half the chopped oysters with their liquid. Cook gently for 10 minutes then add the remaining oysters and ¾ pint of the cream. Simmer for a few minutes to heat through, without boiling. Blend the egg yolks with the remaining cream and stir into the soup. Season. Reheat well through once more but do not boil. Transfer to a warmed tureen, decorate with a sprinkle of cayenne pepper and serve. Serves 4.

Buttered Lobster

Lobster is a delicious luxury and one of the best ways to appreciate its flavour is for it to be cooked and served quite plain without any additional trimmings.

2 medium lobsters, boiled **2 tablespoons double cream**
1½ oz butter **Browned breadcrumbs for topping**

Cut the lobsters in half lengthways, remove all the meat from the shells and claws and cut into chunky pieces. Scrub the empty shells and set aside and keep warm. Melt the butter in a saucepan, add the lobster meat and toss together until heated through. Spoon the meat into the warmed shells. Stir the cream into the pan juices, pour the warm sauce over the lobsters and sprinkle with oven-browned breadcrumbs. Serve hot, at once, on a bed of lettuce with small new potatoes, buttered and garnished with chopped parsley. Serves 4.

Stuffed Gurnard

*This round fish has a large and distinctive head which is left on while cooking.
Traditionally the tail would be curved round and fastened in the mouth.*

2 medium size gurnard   2 – 3 oz melted butter
6 oz forcemeat   4 rashers bacon

FORCEMEAT

4 oz uncooked ham, finely chopped   1 tablespoon finely chopped parsley
2 oz fresh white breadcrumbs   Salt and white pepper
½ beaten egg

First make the forcemeat. Finely chop or mince the ham and combine well with the breadcrumbs and parsley; season and bind with beaten egg. Set oven to 350º F or Mark 4. Clean, de-scale and wash the fish thoroughly, cut off the fins and remove the gills and eyes. Stuff the fish with the forcemeat and sew up or secure with fine skewers. Butter an ovenproof dish, place in it the fish and pour over the remaining melted butter. Lay on the bacon rashers and cover with a lid or foil. Bake for about 40 minutes. Serve hot with parsley or anchovy sauce. Serves 4.

Creamed Prawns

Makes a tasty starter or can be served on toast as a light lunch or supper dish.

8 oz shelled prawns (if frozen, thaw well)   **Salt and white pepper**
4 oz button mushrooms, sliced thinly   **¼ pt milk**
2 oz butter   **¼ pt single cream**
1½ oz wholewheat flour   **3 teaspoons sherry**
Chopped parsley to garnish

Melt the butter in a saucepan and gently fry the mushrooms. Stir in the flour and season with salt and pepper. Stirring continually over a low heat, add the milk and cream and continue stirring until the mixture thickens. Add the prawns and sherry and reheat gently. Put into ramekin dishes, sprinkle with chopped parsley and serve with thin slices of buttered brown bread. Alternatively, serve on slices of buttered toast. Serves 4.

Lyme Bay Fish Pie

Any white fish, or a mixture, can be used with scallops and prawns in this more than ordinary fish pie.

8 oz white fish fillets, skinned and cut into pieces
8 oz scallops (defrost if frozen)
8 oz prawns, cooked and peeled (defrost if frozen)
2 oz butter   6 spring onions, trimmed and sliced   4 oz mushrooms, sliced
1 oz flour   ½ pint fish stock   ¼ pint dry white wine
4 tomatoes, skinned, de-seeded and cut into strips
1 tablespoon chopped parsley   Salt and pepper   8 oz filo pastry

Set oven to 375ºF or Mark 5. Melt 1 oz of the butter in a pan and gently cook the onions and mushrooms for 3 to 4 minutes. Stir in the flour and cook for 2 to 3 minutes more. Remove from the heat and add the stock gradually, stirring well all the time. Stir in the wine. Return to the heat, bring to the boil and cook for 3 to 4 minutes. Remove from the heat, add the fish fillets, scallops, prawns, tomatoes and parsley and season. Put the mixture into a shallow ovenproof dish. Melt the remaining butter. Arrange the sheets of filo pastry on top of the fish, brushing each layer with butter. Trim the pastry and score the surface into diamond shapes. Cook for 25 to 30 minutes until golden. Serve hot. Serves 4.

Durdle Door, Dorset

Shellfish Soup

This recipe takes advantage of the range of frozen shellfish which is available; fresh shellfish can be used where possible.

12 oz mixed shellfish; mussels, scallops, prawns, etc. (defrost if frozen)
2 tablespoons olive oil   2 cloves of garlic, crushed
2 medium onions, diced   1 large tin chopped tomatoes with basil
½ pint dry white wine

Heat the olive oil in a large saucepan and soften the onions and garlic. Add the tinned tomatoes and the wine and cook for 5 minutes. Add the shellfish and cook for a further 5 minutes. Serve piping hot with crusty bread. Serves 4.

Mackerel with Mustard Sauce

Vinegar helps to preserve the oil content of the fish. To prevent the soft flesh from breaking up, simmer only very gently.

4 Mackerel   Vinegar
SAUCE
1 egg   1 tablespoon English mustard powder (or more if preferred)
1 tablespoon sugar   4 tablespoons milk   4 tablespoons vinegar

Carefully gut and clean the fish through as small an incision as possible. Wipe dry and rub each fish with vinegar. Bring a large pan of slightly salted water to the boil. Place the fish on a rack or plate, lower into the water and simmer, very very gently, for 15 minutes. Drain the fish, put on a serving dish and keep warm. SAUCE. Beat the egg in a basin, add the mustard and sugar and mix well. Mix in the milk and vinegar and stand the basin over, but not touching, a pan of simmering water. Stir continually until the sauce thickens. Serve the fish with the hot sauce and with boiled potatoes and a green vegetable. Serves 4.

Roast Sea Bass

This round, somewhat salmon-like fish is caught all round the West Coast of England. Large bass, about 3 to 3½ lbs if available, have the best flavour; the recipe is equally suitable for sea bream.

1 large sea bass or 3 fish approx 1 - 1¼ lb each
3 oz suet   1 tablespoon chopped parsley
4 oz fresh white breadcrumbs   Sea salt
Milk to mix
PARSLEY BUTTER
2 oz butter   1 tablespoon finely chopped fresh parsley

Set oven to 400°F or Mark 6. Clean and de-scale the fish. Keep back 1 oz suet (for basting) and thoroughly mix the rest with the chopped parsley and breadcrumbs and with a pinch of salt. Moisten with a little milk. Stuff the fish with this mixture and put into a greased baking dish. Sprinkle with the remaining suet and season generously with salt. Bake for about 20 to 25 minutes until golden brown, basting frequently and adding more suet if it seems at all dry. Serve with parsley butter made of 2 oz butter and 1 tablespoon finely chopped parsley, well blended together. Serves 3 to 4.

Shrimp and Anchovy Sauce

Fresh peeled shrimps should, ideally, be used for making this accompaniment to sole and shrimp pudding. However they are very fiddly and small frozen prawns can be substituted if preferred.

1 pint basic white sauce
4 - 5 oz shelled shrimps (thaw if frozen)
1 teaspoon lemon juice
1 teaspoon anchovy essence
Cayenne pepper and salt
1 oz butter
2½ fl oz double cream

First make 1 pint of white sauce. To make the sauce, melt 1 oz butter in a pan, stir in 1 oz flour and cook gently for 1 minute, stirring. Remove from the heat and gradually stir in 1 pint milk. Bring slowly to the boil, stirring continually until the sauce thickens then simmer gently for 2 to 3 minutes. Stir into the white sauce the shrimps, lemon juice and anchovy essence. Bring back to the boil and season with Cayenne pepper and salt. Remove from the heat, stir in the butter and double cream and reheat well through but do not allow to boil.

Sole and Shrimp Pudding

A light and fluffy fish and shrimp mould complemented with a shrimp sauce. A luxury, dinner party treat. Small frozen prawns can be used, if preferred.

1½ lb sole fillets	2 egg yolks
2 lb cooked mashed potatoes	1 teaspoon chopped fresh parsley
1 oz butter	Salt and pepper
6 oz Cheddar cheese, grated	1¼ lb shelled shrimps (thaw if frozen)

Parsley sprigs to garnish

Set oven to 350º F or Mark 4. First cook the potatoes then mash and keep warm. Butter a large pudding basin and line with the sole fillets, skin side inwards and tail ends projecting over the edge. Add the butter to the mashed potato and reheat gently, stirring in the grated cheese, egg yolks and parsley and season to taste. Fill the lined mould with alternate layers of potato and shrimps and finally fold over the overlapping sole fillets. Cover with buttered greaseproof paper, place in a *bain marie* and cook in the oven for 40 minutes. Turn out on to a warm serving dish, decorate with parsley sprigs and serve at once with shrimp and anchovy sauce and green peas. Serves 6 to 8.

Buttered Crab

This makes a nice starter; a change from paté.

2 large boiled crabs	½ pint white wine
2 anchovy fillets	Salt and white pepper
1 cup white breadcrumbs	3 tablespoons melted butter
Pinch of nutmeg	Slices of buttered toast

Mash the anchovy fillets and work in with the breadcrumbs and nutmeg. Add the wine and season to taste. Put the mixture into a pan, bring gently to the boil and simmer for 5 minutes. Flake the meat from the crabs, mix with the melted butter and add to the hot wine mixture. Cook gently for 4 minutes then arrange on a hot serving dish surrounded by strips of buttered toast. Serve with a side salad. Serves 6.

Baked Brill

Similar to turbot in flavour and texture, but smaller, brill is particularly good for baking.

4 brill fillets (about 6 oz each) **5 fl oz Madeira or sweet sherry**
Knob of butter **Salt and pepper**
1 oz finely chopped shallots **8 oz fresh white breadcrumbs**
4 oz finely chopped mushrooms **1 teaspoon mixed herbs**
5 fl oz fish stock **2 oz melted butter**
Chopped parsley and cucumber slices to garnish

Set oven to 350° F or Mark 4. Butter an ovenproof dish. First heat a knob of butter in a frying pan and quickly brown the skin side of the brill fillets. Spread the shallots and mushrooms over the bottom of the dish and pour over the stock and wine. Lay the fish on top and season. Mix together the breadcrumbs and herbs and sprinkle over the fish. Pour over the melted butter and cook in the oven for about 30 minutes or until the breadcrumbs have absorbed most of the liquid. Serve garnished with chopped parsley and cucumber slices. Serves 4.

Cream of Scallop Soup

If buying fresh scallops always only select shells that are tightly closed or which close when they are tapped sharply.

24 scallops (thaw if frozen)	**2 oz finely chopped onion**
4 pints fish stock	**2 oz butter**
Salt and pepper	**2 oz flour**
1 bay leaf	**½ pint double cream**
2 cloves	**2 egg yolks**

If using fresh scallops, slide them from the shells, remove the beards and wash and roughly shop the white meat and pink coral. Put the meat and coral into a large saucepan with the stock, bay leaf, cloves and chopped onion and season. Bring to the boil and simmer gently for 20 minutes. Meanwhile, in another pan, make a white roux with the butter and flour and then mix in the strained scallop stock, reserving the strained meat. Bring to the boil, stirring, to thicken and then remove from the heat. Blend together the cream and egg yolks, stir in to the soup and reheat well through but do not allow to boil. Add the reserved scallop meat and allow to warm through just before serving. Serves 6 to 8.

The Cobb, Lyme Regis

Crab Tart

*This savoury tart combines cream cheese and spring onions with the crab meat.
It makes an ideal light lunch or supper dish.*

8 oz shortcrust pastry
FILLING
1/2 - 3/4 lb crab meat (mixture of white and brown meat)

4 oz cream cheese	**2 teaspoons lemon juice**
1 medium egg	**Salt and pepper**
1/4 pint single cream	**4 spring onions, sliced**

Watercress to garnish

Set oven to 400° F or Mark 6. Roll out the pastry on a lightly floured surface and use to line an 8 inch flan ring. Prick the base with a fork, line with cooking foil and bake for 10 to 15 minutes. Remove the foil. For the filling, put the cream cheese into a large bowl and beat until soft. Mix in the egg, cream, lemon juice and seasoning. Arrange the crab meat and the spring onions cut into 1/4 inch slices over the base of the flan and pour over the cheese mixture. Reduce oven to 375°F or Mark 5 and bake for 30 to 40 minutes until set and golden. Serve warm or cold, garnished with watercress. Serves 4.

Sennen Cove Conger Eel

This substantial fish and potato casserole originates from the far west of Cornwall.

2 lb conger eel fillet
1 small onion, finely chopped
2 lb potatoes, peeled and sliced
Salt and pepper
1 tablespoon chopped parsley
1 pint milk
1 teaspoon lemon juice
1 pint fish stock
Chopped fresh parsley for garnish

Skin and bone the eel and wash and dry thoroughly. Cut the flesh into finger size strips. Put the fish pieces into a casserole dish with the chopped onion, cover with the potato slices, season well with salt and pepper and sprinkle over the parsley. Pour over the milk. Mix the lemon juice with 1 pint of fish stock and pour in sufficient of it to cover the contents of the dish. Bring to the boil. Cover and simmer for about 20 minutes until the eel is tender and the potatoes are cooked. Serve garnished with chopped parsley. Serves 4 to 6.

Monkfish Casserole

Only the tails of this ugly, large headed fish are used; the firm, white flesh has a flavour which somewhat resembles that of lobster.

1½ lb monkfish fillet, skinned and cut into cubes

1½ pints dry cider	1 oz flour
1 oz butter	1 tablespoon finely chopped fresh parsley
1 large onion, peeled and diced	1 tablespoon finely chopped marjoram
4 oz button mushrooms	Salt and pepper

2 tablespoons single cream

Set oven to 325° F or Mark 3. Boil the cider rapidly in a saucepan to reduce it to 1 pint. In a separate pan melt the butter, add the onion and cook for about 3 minutes until soft. Add the mushrooms and fish and cook for 1 minute, then add the flour and stir well Pour the reduced cider over the fish, stir well and add the herbs; season to taste. Transfer to an ovenproof dish and bake for 30 minutes (or continue to cook on top of the stove for 30 minutes). Stir in the cream just before serving. Serve with fresh vegetables and crusty bread. Serves 4 to 6.

Dawlish

Crab Soup

This thick purée soup is enriched with cream, as are so many West Country fish dishes.

1 large cooked crab **Salt and pepper**
4 oz long grain rice **Ground nutmeg**
2 pints milk **2 pints chicken stock**
1 oz butter **1 teaspoon anchovy essence**
5 fl oz single cream

Extract all the meat from the crab, keeping the brown and white meat separate. Put the rice, milk and butter into a large saucepan and add salt, pepper and nutmeg to taste. Bring to the boil and then simmer until the rice is tender. Remove from the heat, stir in the brown crab meat and then rub through a sieve or blend in a liquidiser. Return to the pan, add the stock, anchovy essence and the flaked white crab meat. Adjust the seasoning, stir in the cream and reheat the soup well through but do not allow to boil. Serves 6 to 8.

Chesil Beach

METRIC CONVERSIONS

The weights, measures and oven temperatures used in the preceding recipes can be easily converted to their metric equivalents. The conversions listed below are only approximate, having been rounded up or down as may be appropriate.

Weights

Avoirdupois	Metric
1 oz.	just under 30 grams
4 oz. (¼ lb.)	app. 115 grams
8 oz. (½ lb.)	app. 230 grams
1 lb.	454 grams

Liquid Measures

Imperial	Metric
1 tablespoon (liquid only)	20 millilitres
1 fl. oz.	app. 30 millilitres
1 gill (¼ pt.)	app. 145 millilitres
½ pt.	app. 285 millilitres
1 pt.	app. 570 millilitres
1 qt.	app. 1.140 litres

Oven Temperatures

	°Fahrenheit	Gas Mark	°Celsius
Slow	300	2	150
	325	3	170
Moderate	350	4	180
	375	5	190
	400	6	200
Hot	425	7	220
	450	8	230
	475	9	240

Flour as specified in these recipes refers to plain flour unless otherwise described.